SCIENTISTS AT WORK

Dinosaur Hunters
PALEONTOLOGISTS

Richard and Louise Spilsbury

Heinemann Library
Chicago, Illinois

Design: Richard Parker and Manhattan Design
Illustrations: Darren Lingard
Picture Research: Mica Brancic and Virginia Stroud-Lewis
Production: Alison Parsons

Originated by Modern Age
Printed and bound in China by Leo Paper Group

12 11 10 09 08
10 9 8 7 6 5 4 3 2 1

Library of Congress Cataloging-in-Publication Data

Spilsbury, Richard, 1963-
  Dinosaur hunters : paleontologists / Richard and Louise Spilsbury. -- 1st ed.
    p. cm. -- (Scientists at work)
  Includes bibliographical references and index.
  ISBN 978-1-4034-9947-9 (hardback : alk. paper) -- ISBN 978-1-4034-9954-7 (pbk. : alk. paper) 1. Paleontologists--Juvenile literature. I. Spilsbury, Louise. II. Title.
  QE714.7.S65 2007
  560.92--dc22
                            2007012495

Acknowledgments
The publishers would like to thank the following for permission to reproduce photographs: ©Alamy pp. **6** (Stockpile), **13** (Greenshoots Communications); ©Corbis pp. **4**, **19** (Dung Vo Trung), 5 (Danny Lehman), **9** (DK Limited), **10**, **16**, **27** (Jonathan Blair), **12** (Mike Nelson/EPA), **24** (James L Amos), **26** (Ron Watts); ©Getty Images pp. **28** (PhotoDisc), **14**, **15**, **22**, **23**, **25** (Roger Ressmeyer); ©Science Photo library pp. **8** (Ted Clutter), **11** (M-SAT Ltd), **17** (Philippe Plailly/Eurelios), **18** (Pascal Goetgheluck), **20** (Christian Darkin).

Cover photograph of a paleontologist at work reproduced with permission of Science Photo Library/Jim Amos.

The publishers would like to thank Daniel Block for his assistance in the preparation of this book.

Every effort has been made to contact copyright holders of any material reproduced in this book. Any omissions will be rectified in subsequent printings if notice is given to the publishers.

Disclaimer
All the Internet addresses (URLs) given in this book were valid at the time of going to press. However, due to the dynamic nature of the Internet, some addresses may have changed, or sites may have changed or ceased to exist since publication. While the author and publishers regret any inconvenience this may cause readers, no responsibility for any such changes can be accepted by either the author or the publishers.

Contents

Any words appearing in the text in bold, **like this**, are explained in the Glossary.

What Do Paleontologists Do?

Have you seen movies or museum exhibits about dinosaurs? Without paleontologists, we would know very little about these animals or many of the other types of living things that once lived on Earth.

The distant past

Paleontologists study the remains of the animals, plants, and other living things that used to live on Earth. This includes the oldest known **organisms** (living things) from **prehistoric** times, between 3.5 billion and 10,000 years ago. Some types of prehistoric organisms, such as crocodiles and sharks, were very similar to organisms of today. However, other types, such as dinosaurs, are now **extinct**. This means they have all died out.

Sometimes paleontologists find the bones of big dinosaurs. Remains like this help us learn more about extinct animals.

Evidence of the past

Paleontologists piece together the past using **fossils**. Some fossils are remains of parts of plants and animals preserved in rock, such as the curly shells of ancient sea animals called **ammonites**. However, other fossils are indirect clues that prove animals and plants were there. For example, **trace fossils** are remains of burrows or tracks left in sand or soil by prehistoric animals. Other fossils are evidence of things dropped by organisms, such as insect wings, bird feathers, seeds, and even coprolites, which are prehistoric animal feces (droppings).

Paleontologists study the footprints of prehistoric animals to discover where they went, how they moved, and how big they were.

WHO'S WHO: Sue Hendrickson

Sue Hendrickson is a U.S. paleontologist. In August of 1990, Hendrickson was walking her dog during a fossil-hunting expedition, when she noticed some enormous bones sticking out from a cliff. They turned out to be part of the largest *Tyrannosaurus rex* dinosaur skeleton ever found. The skeleton is now on display in the Field Museum in Chicago.

Fossil rocks

Most fossils are found in **sedimentary rocks**, such as sandstone, limestone, and shale rocks. These rocks formed from **particles** or tiny pieces of sand, mud, and broken animal shells. Over time, layers of particles settled in one place and were buried by more particles. When they became pressed together, the particles stuck together, forming flat layers or **strata** of hard rock.

Usually, the remains of ancient organisms that died were eaten or **decomposed** quickly. However, sometimes the remains became buried among the particles. They rotted very slowly when trapped in the rock and gradually turned to fossils in the strata.

Coal is a special sedimentary rock made entirely of fossils. It is formed from remains of ancient, swampy forests. Among the thick black layers of crushed leaves, bark, and wood there are sometimes better preserved fossils of organisms that lived in the forests, such as ferns.

Look at the strata in this cliff. The different layers of rock formed at different times in the past.

Other rocks

Paleontologists generally do not look for fossils in **igneous rocks**, such as granite. These mostly formed when very hot, melted rock or magma from deep inside Earth came to the surface, cooled, and hardened. **Metamorphic rocks** such as marble formed from sedimentary or igneous rocks. The rocks changed after being pressed incredibly hard or heated up underground. Fossils are sometimes found sealed inside metamorphic rocks.

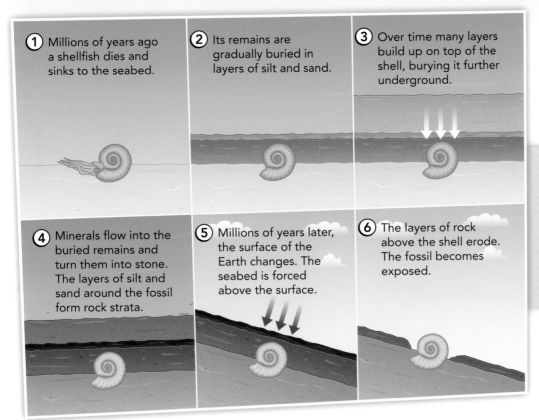

1. Millions of years ago a shellfish dies and sinks to the seabed.

2. Its remains are gradually buried in layers of silt and sand.

3. Over time many layers build up on top of the shell, burying it further underground.

4. Minerals flow into the buried remains and turn them into stone. The layers of silt and sand around the fossil form rock strata.

5. Millions of years later, the surface of the Earth changes. The seabed is forced above the surface.

6. The layers of rock above the shell erode. The fossil becomes exposed.

This diagram shows how a shellfish can turn into a fossil over millions of years.

The science behind it: Turning to stone

Fossilization occurs when water from the surrounding rock flows around the buried organism. The water contains chemicals called **minerals** such as calcium carbonate and silica. They either replace minerals already in the organism or fill up all the tiny spaces within the organism. The minerals turn to hard stone. This process takes hundreds of thousands of years.

Other types of fossils

Have you ever picked up a seashell on a beach? The hard shell is all that is usually left of the organism. The soft flesh inside has been eaten by a seabird or rotted away. Tiny organisms called **bacteria** rot or decompose dead organisms before they can turn into fossils. Hard body parts, such as bones, shells, and teeth, take much longer to decompose than soft parts. Therefore, fossils of these parts are found more often than fossils of softer remains.

Occasionally, fossils of soft organisms are found. These generally form in conditions where there are few bacteria. For example, paleontologists found rare fossils of unusual worms that lived 500 million years ago in the Burgess Shale rocks in Canada. By looking at the rocks, they figured out that the worms died and became buried deep in the ocean where few bacteria live.

These delicate fern leaves were preserved as fossils in ancient peat bogs.

Different fossils

Some fossils are the actual remains of ancient animals. Paleontologists have found bones of extinct animals, such as ground sloths, at the bottom of tar pits. Entire mammoths have been found frozen in ice, and small animals, such as insects, spiders, or frogs, are sometimes found in **amber**. This is tree resin that oozed from the bark of ancient trees, occasionally trapping animals before it hardened.

Paleontologists can see exactly what ancient animals, such as this spider, looked like by examining fossils contained in transparent amber.

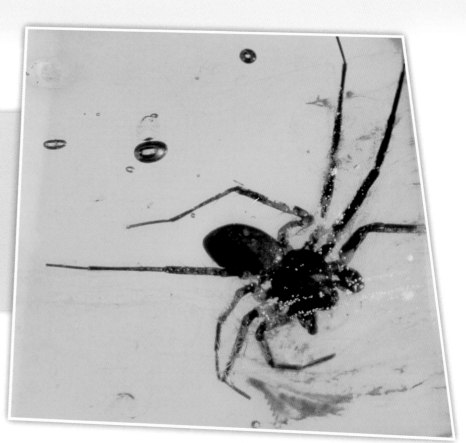

WHO'S WHO: John Merriam

John Merriam is famous for identifying the bones of different animals found in the La Brea tar pits in California. These included saber-toothed cats, which were the size of a lion with teeth 7 inches (17 centimeters) long. These cats may have become trapped in the tar when they came to eat other animals trapped there.

Changing planet

A paleontologist can use fossils to learn what the world was like in the past. For example, paleontologists have found seashell fossils in the Himalayas, which are the highest mountains on Earth. How did they get there? Over time, strata with fossils have been pushed and folded up by movements of rock inside Earth. Some land has risen to form mountains, but other land areas have dropped in level.

The locations of the strata where fossils are found give clues about how Earth has changed since prehistoric times.

Environmental clues

Fossils give us clues about Earth's environment in the past. Fossils of turtles in rock suggest that the area was once a wetland habitat, because this is where similar organisms live today. Some fossils show how the environment within strata changed during formation. Tiny fossil teeth called **conodonts** get darker in color in high temperatures. Scientists have found dark conodonts in rock. This tells them the rock may have once been very hot. When it gets very hot beneath Earth's surface, the remains of ancient sea creatures can turn into oil. This is good news for us because we need the oil to fuel machines.

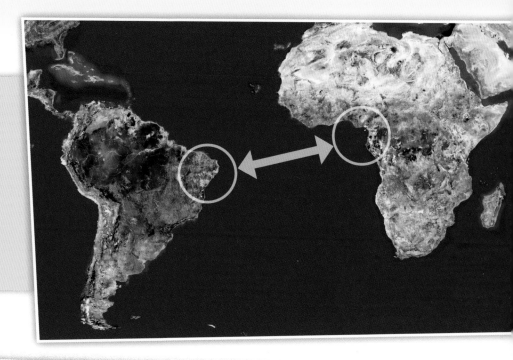

The coastal shapes of western Africa and eastern South America are clues that they were once joined together. Earth's plates later moved them apart.

The science behind it: Moving Earth, changing climate

Paleontologists have found fossils of tropical trees under the thick ice of Antarctica. Today, Antarctica's climate is too cold for many plants to grow. The reason is that the continents on Earth have changed position through time. The surface of the Earth is broken into enormous, thick **plates** or slabs of rock floating on hot, soft rock underneath. In the past, the slab Antarctica is on was closer to the warm equator. Some climate change also happened because of variations of the movement of the Earth around the sun.

How Do Paleontologists Find Fossils?

Fossils can be found anywhere on Earth. Some **sites** (places with many fossils) are discovered accidentally. For example, someone working in a rock quarry may find a fossil when digging up stone for buildings. Fossils can also appear without human assistance. In some cases, rock surfaces may naturally **erode** to reveal the fossils inside.

Paleontologists marked this fossil site with a circle of stones when they last visited so they could find it again.

Finding a site

In most cases, paleontologists have a good idea where to look for fossils. They **excavate** or dig up known fossil sites. They may also use maps to locate sedimentary rocks of a certain age. For example, paleontologists know that dinosaur bones are only found in rocks older than 66 million years. They also look for certain rock formations that are likely to contain fossils. For example, paleontologists might use images taken by **satellites** in space to help search for fossils in a large desert. The images show the type of rock, the shape of the land, and the amount of plants growing in the desert. The paleontologists can then locate eroded, bare sandstone places at the foot of mountains. Ancient sand dunes may once have collapsed there and trapped ancient animals.

Excavation

Paleontologists often work in teams called **field crews** because excavation is slow and tiring. Before starting work, they gather all the equipment they will need. They use pickaxes, hammers, and chisels to chip away hard rock surrounding fossils. They use shovels and trowels to remove the small pieces they have broken off and sometimes to dig into softer rock or loose gravel.

This paleontologist is using a geological pick to remove a fossil from strata. Her helmet is essential protection against falling rocks.

TOOLS OF THE TRADE: EXCAVATION ESSENTIALS

- Geological pick: a special hammer with a pointed end for accurately splitting open rocks
- Safety glasses: to protect eyes from flying rock chips and dust
- Helmet, gloves, kneepads, steel-toed boots: to protect other body parts from rock injuries

Being careful

The workers excavate very carefully so they don't damage fossils as they remove rock and dirt from around them. Sites can be dangerous places. For example, digging a fossil from the base of a cliff could make rock above fall down. They can also be located in hazardous environments, such as baking hot deserts or icy wastelands.

Paleontologists record the location of fossil finds by taking careful field notes and photos. To get an idea of the age of a fossil, they record which strata the fossils are found in. To help determine which fossils lived together in an environment, they record where each fossil was found in the strata.

Paleontologists often sketch what fossils look like in the rock.

Protecting specimens

Even when fossils are made of heavy stone they can still be fragile, especially when they are being removed from rock. Paleontologists often **field jacket** fossils to protect them. They wrap the fossil in damp tissue or aluminum foil and then coat it with strips of burlap cloth dipped in wet plaster of Paris. This hardens around the fossil, just like a plaster cast on a broken bone.

Field crews may need ropes and other lifting equipment to remove heavy fossils from their sites.

WHO'S WHO: Roy C. Andrews

In April of 1922, Roy Andrews led the first paleontological expedition into the Gobi Desert in Asia. The field crew found the first nest of fossil eggs with the skeleton of a small dinosaur on top. Until Andrews' discovery, people had been uncertain whether dinosaur young were born live like mammals or hatched from eggs like reptiles.

Where Do Paleontologists Study Their Finds?

Paleontologists spend much of their time indoors in laboratories instead of outside excavating. This is where they clean, study, and take care of the fossils they find.

Cleaning and preserving

Paleontologists remove field jackets and use water and brushes to wash dirt from fossils. They use special power tools to remove rock. One important tool is an air scribe, which is a miniature version of the jackhammer used to break concrete on roads. Sandblasters are used to shoot particles of hard silica at rock to wear it away. Paleontologists also use dental picks and needles to scratch rock from parts of fossils that are hard to reach. Sometimes they use acids to dissolve rock away (see the box on page 17).

This paleontologist uses a needle to scrape unwanted rock off a 49 million year-old fish fossil.

TOOLS OF THE TRADE: FOSSIL HARDENER

Many fossils seem hard when they are removed from rock, but they are actually quite fragile. Therefore, they need to be preserved. Paleontologists preserve some stone fossils by spraying their surfaces with coats of **consolidant**. This liquid resin soaks into the stone and hardens.

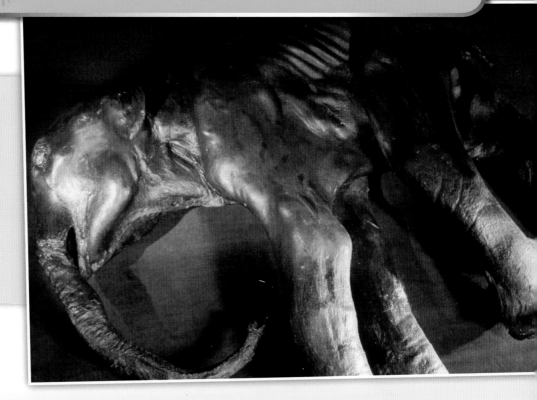

This baby woolly mammoth was found frozen in ice in Eastern Siberia in 1977. Its body was preserved by soaking its skin in wax.

Fossils removed from ice or peat, which is a type of damp soil, are often wet. They are preserved differently from stony fossils. Paleontologists dry these fossils, soak them in special waxes, and keep the air around the fossils cool and dry. This keeps bacteria from destroying the remains.

The science behind it: Disappearing rock

If you put a piece of chalk into a cup of acidic lemon juice or vinegar, it will start to bubble. The chalk is reacting with the acid and changing into carbon dioxide gas and other chemicals. Paleontologists rely on a similar chemical reaction when they use stronger acids to remove limestone from fossils.

Identification

Cleaned fossils are carefully labeled with code numbers. Paleontologists gather field notes, sketches, and photos for the fossil, and give them the same number to show which information belongs to which fossil.

At this stage, paleontologists often have a good idea of the type of organism they have found remains of. They compare the fossil with other fossils, descriptions in books, and living organisms to spot similarities and differences. Sometimes paleontologists identify new types of organisms.

This paleontologist is numbering fossils that were found at a 200,000-year-old cave site in France.

Under the microscope

Some fossils are so tiny they can only be studied under microscopes. These microfossils include conodonts and organisms called diatoms with intricate shapes. Sometimes paleontologists look inside fossils to learn more about them. They use special saws to cut very thin sections of fossils and then look at them under powerful microscopes. For example, leg bones of female dinosaurs are different inside to those of males, so paleontologists can identify the sex of some dinosaurs by looking at bone sections. Cutting sections destroys fossils, so to avoid this they can also see inside using X-rays (see box).

Age

Paleontologists can often tell how old a fossil is by identifying another fossil from the same strata, which they already know the age of. Paleontologists are also able to estimate the age of fossils in one stratum if they know the ages of strata above and below it.

The age of a rock can also be determined by measuring the amounts of certain chemicals. The proportions of these chemicals change over time.

Paleontologists have to use powerful microscopes to get a detailed view of the tiniest fossils.

The science behind it: X-ray view

X-rays are invisible rays that pass through less dense materials but are blocked by denser ones. Paleontologists use photos called radiographs made using X-rays to see, for example, the organs inside a fossil animal or plant.

Paleontologists use fossil finds to bring the past to life. Their studies of fossils add to our knowledge of how the world has changed through time.

Reconstructions

It is rare to find complete remains of organisms, such as an entire skeleton. Usually, paleontologists **reconstruct** how things looked based only on a few body parts. For example, the only remains of the extinct shark megalodon are a few pieces of backbone and its teeth, which are similar in shape to those of a great white shark. Paleontologists estimated that because megalodon's teeth are three times the length of a great white's, then its body may have been three times the length.

This is a reconstruction of how big a megaladon shark was, based on the size of its fossil teeth. A great white shark looks small next to it.

Filling in the gaps

Fossils are like pieces of an enormous, incomplete jigsaw puzzle. Paleontologists ask questions when fossils are not found in specific strata. Does it mean that the organisms were extinct when the rock was formed? Or are there fossils there that have not yet been found? Paleontologists are always searching for more fossils. The more fossils they find, the easier it is to explain why organisms and their environments changed.

This is how a prehistoric fern forest may have looked. It would have smelled of rotting leaves and buzzed with the sound of insects.

The science behind it: Death of the dinosaurs

Dinosaurs were the dominant type of animal on Earth between roughly 200 million and 65 million years ago. No dinosaur fossils younger than that have been found. Many scientists believe that an enormous rock from space hit Earth. The impact changed the climate, and this climate change killed the dinosaurs about 65 million years ago. Scientists believe this because they have found a thin layer of sedimentary rock from roughly 65 million years ago. This rock contains a mineral that isn't normally found on Earth. Scientists think this could have been formed from dust thrown up into the air when the rock hit Earth.

Telling others

When you have discovered something new, you probably want to tell your friends. Paleontologists are just the same. They write reports in journals and give lectures so they can share their work. Other paleontologists may disagree with their findings. For example, in 1999, the fossil of a new birdlike dinosaur was reported in a magazine. Other paleontologists soon realized it wasn't a real fossil. A Chinese farmer had made it in order to sell it.

Many paleontologists work as professors, passing on their knowledge to students. Some also use their knowledge to work with businesses. For example, it is expensive for oil companies to drill for oil. They pay experts on microfossils to study rock samples to make sure they drill in the right places.

One of the best places to see fossil bones is a natural history museum.

Public display

Paleontologists often put fossils on public display. They work with people in charge of museums, national parks, and university fossil collections to make exhibits. They may work with specialized model makers and computer movie makers to create lifelike reconstructions of how ancient organisms looked and lived.

Paleontologists provided expert help when this lifelike *Tyrannosaurus rex* dinosaur was created for the movie *Jurassic Park*.

WHO'S WHO: Jack Horner

In the 1970s, Jack Horner made the discovery that made him famous. He found remains of an unknown type of dinosaur called the *Maiasaura*, along with its nests, eggs, and babies. This proved for the first time that some dinosaurs lived in groups and cared for their young together. The movie maker Steven Spielberg used Horner's dinosaur knowledge to help him make realistic-looking dinosaurs in the movie *Jurassic Park*. He even based the lead paleontologist in the film on Horner.

Paleontologists at work

Hunting for ancient snakes

There is a lot of variety in the job of a paleontologist. There is often no such thing as an "average day." For many paleontologists, their jobs are a mix of fieldwork, research, teaching, and working in the laboratory. They often get to travel around the world in order to carry out fieldwork and meet with other paleontologists.

Mike Caldwell is a Canadian paleontologist who specialises in fossils of reptiles including lizards and snakes. On one trip to South America, he spent time in a museum, looking at new snake fossils. He also gave talks about his research and shared ideas with other paleontologists. Of course, no trip would be complete without going to see the sites where snake fossils have been found. Dr Caldwell's research has taken him to such places as New Zealand, England, Croatia, and Canada. Despite all this he still manages to find time to teach university students!

Paleontologists can be required to work in difficult places. Here, they are uncovering dinosaur bones at the Dinosaur National Monument in Utah.

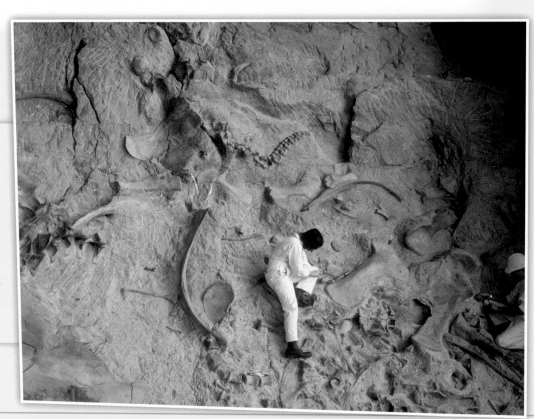

Revealing the past

There are many different jobs within the field of paleontology. One of the most important is that of fossil preparator. Their job is to expose the information that is in a fossil for scientists to see and study. Marilyn Fox is a fossil preparator at the Peabody Museum of Natural History. A typical day in her working life might be patiently scraping tiny flecks of rock from fossil bones or removing fossil eggshells to reveal baby dinosaurs inside. Sometimes, when starting on a project, she has no idea what sort of creature she will find.

On other days Fox may make plaster cast models of fragile fossils for other paleontologists to study, or mend old fossils in the museum's collection. The job takes great skill and attention to detail. At museums, thousands of people look at the work of fossil preparators every day.

Fossil preparators work patiently to get fossils ready for display to the public and to other paleontologists.

What Does It Take To Be a Paleontologist?

Fossil displays like this can really help students get an idea of what extinct animals looked like and how they lived at different times.

Learning more

Are you interested in becoming a paleontologist? You may already like to find fossils and have a collection of your finds. Perhaps you enjoy visiting exhibits, reading books, and watching movies about prehistoric life. It is a good idea to follow your interests, but it is also important to study hard at school. Many subjects are useful to a fossil hunter, such as geography to learn about different places in the world. History can help us understand the past, while art can teach us how to draw reconstructions of extinct organisms. But the most useful subjects are sciences.

Paleontologists mostly study science subjects at a university or college. Biology is important in order to learn about organisms. Geology is the study of rock types, how they formed, and how they have changed over time. Successful students get qualifications such as college degrees to help them get paleontology jobs.

Specializing

Many paleontologists have a specific interest in certain types of remains. The three broad specializations are paleozoology (the study of prehistoric animals), paleobotany (the study of prehistoric plants), and micropaleontology (the study of microfossils such as bacteria, conodonts, and pollen). Some paleontologists just study specific types of animals, while others may study just fossils of certain ages.

Sharing their findings with other people, including students, is an important part of a paleontologist's job.

WHO'S WHO: Mike Newman

Not all adult fossil hunters are paleontologists. Some do it as a hobby. For example, Scottish bus driver Mike Newman is a fossil hunter. In 2004 Newman found the remains of a millipede that was 428 million years old. It is the oldest fossil of a land animal ever found.

Timeline

1920s: Clumps of fossil bacteria called stromatolites are found by Rob Ritchie in New York

1830s: Abraham Gesner finds fossil trees in coal, in Joggins, Nova Scotia

Precambrian Era

3500–590 million years ago
Fossils show: all organisms lived in oceans and ranged from tiny bacteria to sponges and flat worms.

Early Paleozoic Era

590–409 million years ago
Fossils show: most organisms were ocean invertebrates, such as trilobites. Vertebrates included sharks.

Late Paleozoic Era

408–249 million years ago
Fossils show: there were many plants and animals, from ferns and trees to insects and reptiles, on land.

1909: Burgess Shale is found. It contains many soft-bodied animal fossils.

2004: Mike Newman finds a fossil millipede (see page 27)

1667: Niels Stensen realizes that tongue stones on a beach look like shark teeth because they are fossil remains

1823: Fossil bones of a mammoth are found with those of humans in a British cave, proving they lived on Earth at the same time

1997: Complete mammoth is found in ice in Siberia in Asia

Mesozoic Era

248–66 million years ago
Fossils show: dinosaurs ruled the Earth, many ammonites lived in the oceans, and the first flowering plants and mammals developed on land.

Cenozoic Era

65 million years ago—today
Fossils show: there are many types of mammals, including humans, along with numerous insects, fish, flowers, and other organisms.

1795: Georges Cuvier identifies reptile bones from a quarry as those of an extinct dinosaur

1802: Pliny Moody finds fossil footprints on his family farm

1905: *Tyrannosaurus rex* is named and described in the United States

1922: Roy Andrews finds dinosaur egg fossils (see page 15)

1980: Scientists find a clay layer that supports the idea of dinosaur extinction by asteroid (see page 21)

1990: Sue Hendrickson finds the biggest *T. rex* skeleton (see page 5)

Glossary

amber fossilized tree sap, often found with fossilized animals inside

ammonite snail-like fossil invertebrate that lived in oceans 400 million to 65 million years ago

bacteria microscopic organisms, some of which decompose dead organisms and waste

conodont microscopic teeth of small wormlike creatures also called conodonts

consolidant liquid plastic used to harden fossils and other soft rocks

decompose rot or break down. Organisms decompose over time.

erode wear away rocks or soil

excavate dig up fossils from the ground

extinct a type of organism is extinct when all of them have died out completely

field crew group of workers on a paleontological or other dig

field jacket to wrap fragile fossils in a plaster cast in order to strengthen them; can also mean the plaster cast itself

fossil remains of organisms that lived in the prehistoric past

igneous rock rock formed by cooling of hot, liquid rock from deep underground

metamorphic rock rock changed by heat and pressure deep underground

minerals natural chemicals that are the building blocks of rock

organism living animal or plant

particle very tiny piece or amount

plate section of Earth's outer layer of rock. The Earth is made up of several plates that move slowly around the globe.

prehistoric from the period of time before written records, before roughly 10,000 years ago

reconstruct rebuild or make something look like an object from the past

satellite human-made machine designed to travel around Earth or other objects in space

sedimentary rock rock formed in strata from particles of sand and mud that built up, for example in ancient seas

site place with many fossils or other things of interest

strata layers of rock formed at different times

trace fossil remains of activities of ancient organisms, such as footprints

Find Out More

Further reading

Hendrickson, Sue. *Hunt for the Past: My Life as an Explorer*. New York: Scholastic, 2001.

Larson, Peter, and Kristin Donnan. *Bones Rock!: Everything You Need to Know To Be a Paleontologist*. Montpelier, VT.: Invisible Cities Press, 2004.

Morgan, Ben. *Rock and Fossil Hunter (Nature Activities)*. New York: Dorling Kindersley, 2005.

Padma, T.V. *The Albertosaurus Mystery: Philip Currie's Hunt in the Badlands*. New York: Bearport Publishing Company, 2007.

Quigley, Mary. *Dinosaur Digs*. Chicago: Heinemann Library, 2006.

Taylor, Paul. *Fossils (Eyewitness Guide)*. New York: Dorling Kindersley, 2003.

Websites

Find out about the work of real-life paleontologist, Paul Sereno. Learn all about expeditions and dinosaur discoveries, including supercroc, an enormous crocodile that ate dinosaurs. There are even pictures of Paul's fossil lab:
http://www.paulsereno.org

Artist John Payne uses science and art to create his dinosaur sculptures and to make them move:
http://www.childrensmuseum.org/special_exhibits/kinetosaur/index.html

Go on an interactive virtual dinosaur dig at:
http://www.nmnh.si.edu/paleo/dinosaurs/interactives/dig/dinodig.html

San Diego Natural History Museum's website defines fossils and describes the best places to look for fossils. Find the Fossil Mysteries pages and check out pictures of megalodon and the clay layer of the K-T boundary, when dinosaurs became extinct at:
http://www.sdnhm.org/kids/fossils/index.html

Index